A New Approach to
Sight Singing

▨ FOURTH EDITION ▨ ▨ ▨ ▨ ▨ ▨ ▨ ▨ ▨ ▨ ▨ ▨

A New Approach to
Sight Singing

 **FOURTH EDITION**

Sol Berkowitz *Professor of Music*

Gabriel Fontrier *Professor Emeritus of Music*

Leo Kraft *Professor Emeritus of Music*

The Aaron Copland School of Music at
Queens College of the City University of New York

 W. W. NORTON & COMPANY *New York / London*

ACKNOWLEDGMENTS

Bartók, Bagatelle, Op. 6, No. 6 (p. 298): Used by permission of Boosey & Hawkes, Inc.

Prokofiev, *Lieutenant Kije Suite* (pp. 280, 286, 289): Used by permission of Boosey & Hawkes, Inc.

Prokofiev, *Peter and the Wolf* (pp. 282, 293): Copyright © 1937, 1940 (Renewed) by G. Schirmer, Inc. (ASCAP) throughout the United States, Canada, and Mexico. International Copyright Secured. All Rights Reserved. Reprinted by Permission.

Schoenberg, *Transfigured Night* (p. 297): Used by permission of Belmont Music Publishers, Pacific Palisades, CA 90272.

Shostakovich, Symphony No. 1, I (p. 297): Copyright © 1927 (Renewed) by G. Schirmer, Inc. (ASCAP) throughout the United States, Canada, and Mexico. International Copyright Secured. All Rights Reserved. Reprinted by Permission.

R. Strauss, *Don Juan* (p. 281): By permission of G. Schirmer, Inc.

Stravinsky, *The Firebird* (p. 295): By permission of G. Schirmer, Inc.

Stravinsky, *Petrushka* (pp. 277, 285, 285): © Copyright 1912 by Hawkes & Son (London) Ltd.; Copyright Renewed. New Version © Copyright 1948 by Hawkes & Son (London) Ltd.; Copyright Renewed. Used by permission of Boosey & Hawkes, Inc.

Stravinsky, *The Rite of Spring* (pp. 287, 298): © Copyright 1912, 1921 by Hawkes & Son (London) Ltd. Used by permission of Boosey & Hawkes, Inc.

Stravinsky, *L'Histoire du Soldat* (p. 291): By permission of G. Schirmer, Inc.

The text of this book is composed in Palatino with the display set in Helvetica

Music typography and composition by David Budmen, Willow Graphics, Woodstown, New Jersey

Book design by Andy Zutis

Library of Congress Cataloging-in-Publication Data

Berkowitz, Sol.
   A new approach to sight singing / Sol Berkowitz, Gabriel Fontrier, Leo Kraft.—4th ed.
      p. cm.
   ISBN 0-393-96908-8 (pbk.)
      1. Sight-singing.   I. Frontrier, Gabriel.   II. Kraft, Leo.
MT870.B485N5   1997
783'.0423—dc20   96-31963

W. W. Norton & Company, Inc., 500 Fifth Avenue, New York, N.Y. 10110
            http://www.wwnorton.com
W. W. Norton & Company Ltd., 10 Coptic Street, London, WC1A 1PU

   6 7 8 9 0

To John Castellini,
our teacher, our good friend and colleague, our editor,
this book is affectionately dedicated.

Contents

Preface to the Fourth Edition

About This Book

This book consists of a coordinated body of musical materials specifically composed for the study of sight singing, as well as a new chapter of melodies from the standard classical and folk repertories. A mastery of sight singing is essential to the performer, the scholar, the composer, the teacher—to any musician or intelligent amateur. In an ideal world, instrumental and vocal students would be taught to sing at sight from the beginning of their training, but in reality very few receive such instruction. Training in sight singing often lags behind training in performance and academic studies. Courses in sight singing, therefore, have become an essential part of the curricula of secondary schools, conservatories, colleges, and universities.

While most current texts offer only melodies from the literature, not created specifically for pedagogical purposes, *A New Approach to Sight Singing* has consisted of music newly composed to provide graded material for sight singing classes. Exercises written for classroom use formed the basis for previous editions of this book. Drawing on the experience of four decades of teaching as well as on valuable comments from other users of the book, for this edition we have written new material, refined some of the exercises, deleted some others, and added a completely new chapter.

Melodies from the Literature

Prompted by our own teaching experience and the much appreciated suggestions of many colleagues, we have added a new Chapter Five, "Melodies from the Literature," to the fourth edition. While the chapters carried over from previous editions are en-

tirely our own material, this new chapter provides melodies from the standard repertory, together with folk material. Study of these melodies will enable students to make the transfer of learning from exercises to the music with which they will be working during their professional lives. The melodies in Chapter Five were chosen to represent a wide variety of musical styles, both vocal and instrumental. A few have been adapted for sight singing purposes. The level of difficulty of each section within Chapter Five corresponds to the comparable level within the other chapters. Attributions are given for each melody.

Organization of the Book

The fourth edition consists of five chapters, as well as supplementary exercises, two appendices, and a newly added page of "warm-ups" at the beginning of Chapter One. Chapter One contains unaccompanied melodies and is the core of the book. Chapter Two presents vocal duets. Chapter Three contains melodies with piano accompaniment, including accompanied variation sets. Chapter Four presents unaccompanied themes and variations. The new Chapter Five offers melodies from the literature, drawn from both the written and oral traditions. The supplementary exercises contain specific drills in scales and chords, chromatic notes of all kinds, and advanced rhythmic problems. Appendix I is a glossary of musical terms used in the text, which includes most terms in current use. Appendix II explains some frequently used musical signs.

In each chapter there are four sections: Section I is at the elementary level, Sections II and III, intermediate, and Section IV, advanced. Assuming two class meetings a week, each section corresponds to one semester's work, about thirty class hours. The material of each section is graded progressively. The unit of work is the Section. Section I materials in each of the five chapters make up a coordinated body of exercises to be used concurrently, sufficient for one semester. The same applies to Sections II, III, and IV.

A Typical Class

Beginning students start with the first section of each chapter. A freshman class hour might begin with singing a group of melodies from Chapter One, Section I. The class could then turn to the duets of Chapter Two, again using Section I; the unaccompanied melodies of Chapter Three, Section I; one of the variation sets in Chapter Four, Section I; or melodies from the literature, Chapter Five, Section I. Much of the class time will probably be devoted to singing melodies, which comprise over half of the book. But frequent use of Chapters Two, Three, Four, and Five opens up different approaches to the subject, offers a desirable change of pace within the class hour, and also shows how skills acquired in one area may be applied to other musical situations.

Place in the Curriculum

A New Approach to Sight Singing is so organized that it may be adapted to different programs of study. Being essentially diatonic, Sections I and II may readily be integrated with the study of diatonic harmony and counterpoint, while Sections III and IV may be coordinated with the study of chromatic harmony.

This book offers a large body of materials and there is no expectation that all will be used by every instructor. Rather, we offer as generous a number of choices as is practical. Each instructor will stress those aspects of sight singing that seem appropriate to a particular class of aspiring musicians at a particular school, drawing upon the various materials in the several chapters in the way that seems most applicable to the teaching situation.

Topic Headings

As an aid to organizing the course, the specific tech-

nical problems introduced in Chapter One are identified by brief headings, each followed by a short group of melodies that focuses on the topic at hand. Immediately after, there is a longer group of melodies combining all topics introduced up to that point.

The Five Chapters

A brief summary of each chapter will give an overview of the book's organization:

The melodies in Chapter One, Section I introduce technical problems progressively: while the first tunes are simple and quite short, later ones gradually increase in length and complexity. These melodies are diatonic, emphasizing fundamental aspects of tonality. Stepwise motion, skips based on familiar chord outlines, and basic rhythmic patterns are presented here. A group of modal melodies concludes this section.

The melodies of Section II, while largely diatonic, introduce a few chromatic notes, as well as simple modulation to the dominant or relative major, together with some larger skips and slightly more complex rhythms.

Section III includes more chromaticism and additional modulations. Melodies are longer, phrase structures more complex, and rhythms more diverse. Chapter One, Section IV offers more challenging exercises in tonality as well as in rhythm, meter, and phrasing; dynamics, phrase structure, and musical interpretation are on a more sophisticated level. The section concludes with material based on twentieth-century idioms. Treble, alto, and bass clefs are found in all sections; the tenor clef is introduced in Section IV.

The purpose of Chapter Two, "Duets," is to develop skill in ensemble singing. Students not only sing their own part but also listen to another, sung by a different voice. The duets may also be given as prepared assignments; many colleagues have found them useful for class dictation.

Experience has strengthened our conviction that the piano is essential in developing musicianship. Chapter Three affords opportunities to develop that musicianship by playing one part while singing another. In doing so the student improves the ability to hear, while also developing good intonation and sharpening rhythmic skills. "Sing and Play" also offers an effective way to study the relationship between harmony and melody. This chapter now includes variation sets with piano accompaniment. While the instructor may ask some students to perform "Sing and Play" exercises at sight, these will most often be given as homework. We recommend an assignment from Chapter Two every week.

"Themes and Variations," Chapter Four, offers relatively extended compositions, which may be sung entirely by one student or divided among several. Because the character of the music changes from one variation to another, the student is stimulated to think about matters of musical interpretation.

In response to suggestions from colleagues throughout the country and in accordance with our own desire to add this dimension to the book, we have prepared Chapter Five, which includes melodies from the standard repertory and from the folk music of many cultures. Used in tandem with the other chapters, these melodies provide a transition from our exercises to traditional literature. Written originally for instruments or voice, the melodies in this new chapter offer a rich diversity of musical styles.

Additional Uses of This Book

The Supplementary Exercises provide an assortment of drills in intervallic relationships, skips of all kinds, intonation, and rhythm. Part I of the Supplementary Exercises is to be used with Sections I and II of the five chapters, while Part II is to be used with Sections III and IV.

This book has been used in a number of ways, including classroom dictation. The duets have been proven particularly valuable for that purpose. Those wishing to find a way of developing hearing skills outside the classroom may consult Leo Kraft's *A New Approach to Ear Training*.* An excellent way for students to continue work on their own is to write down melodies that they know or have heard recently, or to which they have access through recordings. It is also quite valuable to play familiar music by ear on the piano or another instrument.

Acknowledgments

We take this opportunity to express our appreciation and thanks to the many generation of Queens College students whose responses to our book have helped shape our thinking and who have taught us so much. We are also grateful for suggestions from colleagues both on our own campus and beyond it, especially in the selection of examples from the literature.

We are especially indebted to Professor John Castellini, our patient and devoted editor, who continuously labored with our manuscript and helped define its final form. Many of our basic ideas concerning music and music theory were gained during our years as students and colleagues of the late Karol Rathaus. To him, then, we owe a special debt of gratitude.

Beyond that, the widespread favorable reaction to the first three editions has encouraged us to continue our search for as many approaches to sight singing as we can create.

Everyone can learn to sing and to enjoy singing. No matter what kind of voice one possesses, competence in singing can be achieved by consistent practice. The satisfaction thus gained will more than justify the effort of time expended. To be sure, sight singing is not an end in itself: it opens the door to musical experiences of many kinds. The ability to sing melodies at sight is also one of the necessary skills that a good musician must possess. Music does not live on paper. To bring it to life there must be an instrument that can sing, an ear that can hear, and a musical mind that can sing and hear in the silence of thought.

Berkowitz / Fontrier / Kraft
Queens College 1996

---

*New York: W. W. Norton, 1967.

A New Approach to
Sight Singing

FOURTH EDITION

CHAPTER ONE

Melodies

Before singing a melody (or performing music of any sort) it is necessary to understand thoroughly the system of music notation we use today. The five-line staff with the clef signs, time signatures, tempo indications, and expression markings constitute a musical code, all the elements of which must be decoded simultaneously in order to transform what has been set down on paper into music.

Establish the Key

The melodies in Section I are tonal. Each is written in a specific key and the student must establish that key before attempting to sing. The tonic note of the key (rather than the first note of the melody) should be played on the piano or the pitch pipe and sung by the student. Then the scale of the key should be sung, ascending and descending, after which an arpeggio consisting of tonic, 3rd, 5th, and octave may be sung to establish further a feeling for the tonality of the melody.

Establish the Tempo

Next it is necessary to take cognizance of the tempo (rate of speed) and the meter (number of beats to the measure). Many different tempo indications have been used in this book to familiarize the student with most of the terms in common use. It is important that the singer know the meaning of these tempo markings, all of which are to be found in the Glossary (page 325).

The time signature denotes meter. Simple meters (duple, triple, and quadruple) are indicated by signatures having a 2, 3, or 4 as the upper numeral, or by the signs C (corresponding to $\frac{4}{4}$ meter) or ¢ (*alla breve*, corresponding to $\frac{2}{2}$ meter). Regular compound meters ($\frac{6}{8}$, $\frac{9}{8}$, and $\frac{12}{8}$) are combinations of simple meters within one measure.

Tempo can be established and meter defined by the student if he beats time as a conductor does. Standard conducting patterns should be used consistently. $\frac{6}{8}$ time may be conducted in six or in two beats; $\frac{9}{8}$ and $\frac{12}{8}$ time in separate beats or in three or four beats respectively. Tempo, and often the character of a melody, will serve the student in determining how to conduct compound meters.

Singing Melodies Without Texts

It is advisable to sing some definite syllable for every note the better to control quality and intonation. In many foreign countries *solfeggio* (the application of the *sol-fa* syllables to the degrees of the scale) is used in sight singing. This practice is officially sanctioned by foreign national conservatories. In our country, however, several methods of singing melodies without texts are in common use. These may be summarized as follows:

Fixed *Do*

In the fixed *Do* system, our notes, C, D, E, F, G, A, and B, are called *Do, Re, Mi, Fa, Sol, La,* and *Ti*. In singing a melody, the name for each note is sung without regard to any accidental. Countries which use this technique have been quite successful with it, perhaps because of the rigorous early training which their students receive.

Movable *Do*

In the movable *Do* system, *Do* always represents the tonic or first degree of the scale, regardless of key. Accidentals are accounted for by changing the syllables. The ascending chromatic scale reads as follows: *Do, Di, Re, Ri, Mi, Fa, Fi, Sol, Si, La, Li, Ti, Do.* The descending chromatic scale reads as follows: *Do, Ti, Te, La, Le, Sol, Se, Fa, Mi, Me, Re, Ra, Do.*

When a melody modulates, the new tonic is called *Do*, and the other notes of the scale are renamed accordingly. The purpose of this system is to emphasize the relationship between the degrees of the scale, and to develop a feeling for tonality even when the tonal center shifts.

Other Methods

Numbers (1, 2, 3, etc.) may be used instead of syllables (*Do, Re, Mi*, etc.). The application is the same as in the movable *Do* system except that there is no numeral change for chromatic tones.

One syllable, such as *la*, may be used for all pitches. Thus the singer does not have to translate the pitch names into syllables or numbers.

A musician is expected to know the system in common use wherever he may be; therefore, the student should master more than one of these techniques.

Phrasing

The student is urged to avoid note-to-note singing and to make a genuine effort to grasp an entire phrase as a musical entity. To guide and encourage this process of looking ahead, slurs and articulation markings have been placed over the phrases of every melody. These indications define the phrase structure and serve as a guide to breathing.

Musical Values

In practicing the singing of melodies, as in practicing an instrument, the beginner may be tempted to concentrate on producing the correct pitch, hoping that other musical values will be acquired in due course. But melodies do not exist without rhythm; they also have nuances of dynamics and tempo, and climaxes. These qualities are an integral part of the music. It is possible to improve one's musicianship while learning the technique of sight singing by thinking about musical values with the first melody in the book. As an aid to intelligent and sensitive performance we have included dynamics, expression, and articulation markings throughout the book. The eye should be trained to observe them; the mind to implement them.

Prepare to Sing

Clearly, there is much to do, and it is suggested that the student "make haste slowly." The first melodies should be studied carefully in order to develop good musical habits. The student should sing a melody several times, if necessary, until ease and fluency are achieved.

Before you start to sing, we suggest that you:

- Look at the melody quickly (scan it): where are the high and low points?
- Look for dynamic marks and articulation.
- Sing an arpeggio that fits the range of the melody.
- Sing one or more of the following warm-ups in the key and tempo of the exercise.
- It is helpful to beat time as you sing, using standard conducting patterns.

Here are some suggested warm-ups:

Warm-ups

MELODIES ▨ **SECTION I**

To be used with Section I of all other chapters

The first melodies emphasize the basic aspects of tonality. They are designed to include easily recognizable scale and chordal patterns. These diatonic melodies are based on both major and minor modes.

The phrases are usually symmetrical and short enough to be grasped at a glance. However, the diversity of rhythms, keys, modes, tempos, dynamics, and clefs should provide a variety of musical experiences. The alto clef is introduced in exercise 33b; the minor mode in 47; compound meter § in 59c.

▨ ▨ ▨ The first eight melodies are based entirely on stepwise motion. The largest range is a single octave. Note values include o ♩ ♪ ♫. All of these melodies begin with the root of the tonic triad. Each of the first eight melodies is in one phrase.

1. *Andante*

2. *Allegretto*

3. *Allegro*

4. *Andante cantabile*

5. *Allegro*

6. *Largo*

7. *Andantino*

8. *Allegretto*

 Each of the next four melodies is built in two phrases. Scan the melody for the peak of each phrase.

9. *Con moto*

10. *Allegro*

11. *Allegro*

12. *Allegro deciso*

The pattern of two short phrases and one longer one is found in the next three melodies.

13. *Allegretto*

14. *Allegro*

15. *Andante*

 The following nine melodies introduce skips in the tonic triad.

16. *Allegro*

17. *Andante con moto*

18. *Vivace*

19. *Allegretto*

20. *Allegro moderato*

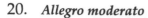

21. *Allegro con brio*

22. *Allegro molto*

23. *Allegro*

24. *Allegretto*

The rhythm ♩. ♪ is included in the next five melodies.

25. *Allegro moderato*

26. *Allegro*

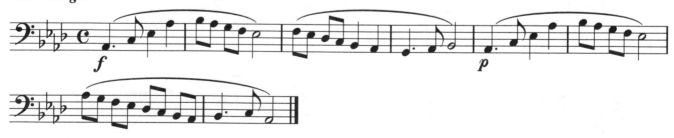

27. *Vivace*

28. *Andante*

29. *Andante*

30. *Allegro*

31. *Vivace*

32. *Andante cantabile*

▧ ▨ ▧ The same melody is written with three different clefs.

33a. *Moderato*

33b. *Moderato*

33c. *Moderato*

▧ ▨ ▧

▧ ▨ ▧ The next ten melodies are written using the alto clef.

34. *Andante*

35. *Largo*

36. *Allegretto*

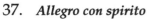

37. *Allegro con spirito*

44. *Andante*

45. *Moderato con moto*

a tempo

46. *Allegro con spirito*

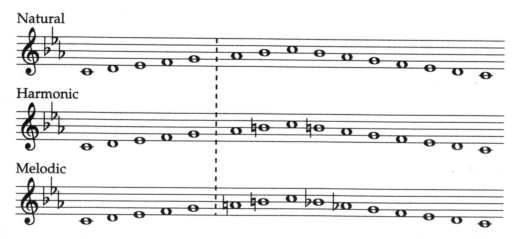

Three C-minor scales.

Natural

Harmonic

Melodic

Melodies in which the major and minor modes are compared may be found in Supplementary Exercises, p. 301ff.

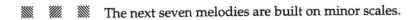 The next seven melodies are built on minor scales.

47. *Andante*

48. *Allegro*

49. *Andantino*

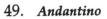

50. *Allegro*

51. *Allegro moderato*

52. *Andante*

53. *Allegretto*

 Skips in the tonic minor triad are found in the next four melodies.

54. *Andante*

55. *Allegro*

56. *Allegretto*

57. *Moderato*

58. *Allegretto*

The same melody is notated in three different meters.

59a. *Moderato*

59b. *Allegro*

59c. *Larghetto*

The next eight melodies are in ⅜ time. Observe the differences between two versions of the same melody, given in different modes.

60. *Andantino*

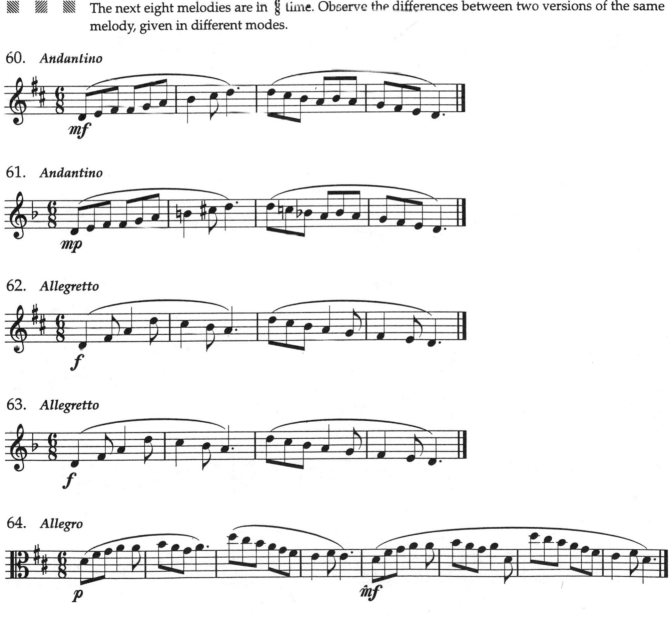

61. *Andantino*

62. *Allegretto*

63. *Allegretto*

64. *Allegro*

65. Allegro

66. Con anima

67. Con anima

Rests are included in some melodies from this point on.

68. Allegro moderato

69. Andante cantabile

70. Allegro

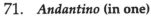

71. *Andantino* **(in one)**

72. *Allegro*

 The next four melodies begin with the 5th of the tonic triad.

73. *Allegro*

74. *Larghetto*

75. *Andante*

76. *Andante pastorale*

The next three melodies begin with the 3rd of the tonic triad.

77. *Allegro*

78. *Andantino*

79. *Allegro con spirito*

80. *Andante*

81. *Frisch und munter*

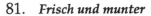

▨ ▨ ▨ The next four melodies begin with ♩ upbeats.

82. *Allegro moderato*

83. *Andantino*

84. *Tempo di menuetto*

85. *Andantino*

▨ ▨ ▨

▨ ▨ ▨ The next ten melodies include skips in the IV chord, in both major and minor.

86. *Andante*

100. *Moderato*

101. *Allegro*

102. *Andante con moto*

103. *Scherzando*

104. *Tempo di menuetto*

105. *Con moto*

106. *Allegro*

107. *Assez lent*

108. *Allegro deciso*

109. *Langsam*

110. *Andante con moto*

111. *Allegro deciso*

112. *Larghetto*

The next five melodies include skips in the V chord, in both major and minor.

113. *Vif et léger*

114. *Vif et léger*

115. *Andante*

116. *Andante*

117. *Mässig*

124. *Moderato*

125. *Animato*

126. *Ben ritmico*

127. *Adagietto*

128. *Valse*

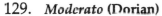 Section I concludes with a group of melodies based on these four modes.

Dorian   Mixolydian

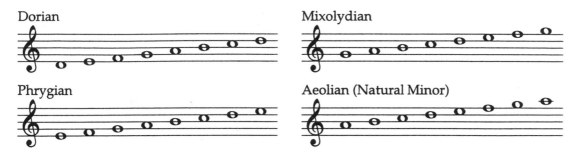

Phrygian   Aeolian (Natural Minor)

129. *Moderato* **(Dorian)**

p

130. *Andante* **(Dorian)**

mf   *f*   *p*

131. *Andante con moto* **(transposed Dorian)**

p

132. *Lento* **(Phrygian)**

p   *mp*   *p*

133. *Andante con moto* **(Phrygian)**

f

134. *Moderato con moto* **(Phrygian)**

135. *Allegro* **(transposed Phrygian)**

136. *Mässig* **(Mixolydian)**

137. *Allegro non troppo* **(Mixolydian)**

138. *Vivement* **(transposed Mixolydian)**

139. *Moving forward* (Aeolian)

p

140. *Lento* (Aeolian)

p   pp   p   mp   pp   p

141. *Andante sostenuto* (transposed Aeolian)

mf

p   dim.   *rall.*

MELODIES ▨ *SECTION II*

To be used with Section II of all other chapters

These melodies contain simple modulations, more complex rhythms, and diatonic skips in a variety of contexts. As in Melodies, Section I, the tonality of each melody is clearly defined. Some phrases are longer; some are less symmetrical; syncopations are introduced; and the vocal range is extended.

▨ ▨ ▨   The next six melodies introduce skips in the V⁷ chord, in both major and minor.

142. *Andante*

143. *Andante*

144. *Andante con moto*

145. *Langsam*

146. *Allegretto*

147. *Andante*

153. *Ballando*

The next five melodies introduce less frequently used meters: $\frac{3}{8}$, $\frac{9}{8}$, $\frac{12}{8}$, and $\frac{6}{4}$.

154. *Andante cantabile*

155. *Doux et expressif*

156. *Larghetto*

157. *Pastorale*

158. *Andante con moto*

mf *p* *mf* *p*

Triplets are included in the next three melodies.

159. *Maestoso*

f

160. *Largo*

p

161. *Andante con moto*

p

162. *Andante*

163. *Ziemlich schnell*

 Skips of all diatonic intervals up to an octave are included from this point on.

164. *Andante con moto*

165. *Lentement*

166. *Langsam*

⬚ ⬚ ⬚ Ties are included in many of the melodies from this point on.

167. *Allegretto*

168. *Andante*

169. *Vivace*

170. *Allegro*

171. *Allegro*

172. *Alla marcia*

173. *Andante*

 The next six melodies begin with upbeats ♪ or ♫.

174. *Allegro marziale*

Syncopations are introduced in the next six melodies.

180. *Allegro*

181. *Sustained*

182. *Gaio*

183. *Largo*

184. *Lively*

185. *Brisk*

191. *Allegro*

192. *Valse* **(in one)**

193. *Andantino grazioso*

▨ ▨ ▨ The next four melodies include chromatic neighbor notes.

194. *Andante*

195. *Andante*

196. *Andantino piacevole*

197. *Moderato*

198. *Mässig und zart*

199. *Lively*

200. *Moderato con moto*

201. *Allegretto*

202. *Cheerful*

The next four melodies, in the minor mode, move through the relative major. Before singing, find the point where that motion begins.

203. *Allegro*

204. **Allegro moderato**

205. **Larghetto**

206. **Andantino**

207. **Andante**

208. *Waltz tempo*

209. *Allegro moderato*

▧ ▧ ▧ The next three melodies include chromatic passing notes.

210. *Moderato con moto*

211. *Andante con moto*

212. *Allegro non troppo*

213. *Lilting*

214. *Ben ritmico*

215. *Maestoso*

216. *Animé*

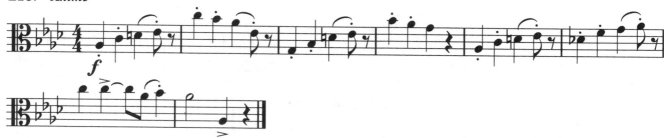

217. *Lento*

218. *Slowly*

219. *Andante con moto*

The next three melodies, in the major mode, move through the dominant.

220. *Allegretto grazioso*

221. *Fanfare*

222. *Allegro assai*

223. *Allegro e ben marcato*

224. *Allegro gioviale*

225. *Andantino*

226. *Allegro moderato*

D. C. al Fine

p subito

227. *Minuet*

228. *Modéré*

229. *Allegro gioviale*

230. *Briskly*

231. *Etwas gedehnt*

232. *Allegro lunatico*

233. *Scherzando*

MELODIES ▓ SECTION III

To be used with Section III of all other chapters

Chromatic alterations are used with increasing frequency in melodies of this section. Some indicate modulation; some are factors in secondary dominant harmonies; others are melodic embellishments. Within these melodies there is an increasing diversity of rhythms, intervals, phrase structures, and musical styles.

The material of Section III can readily be correlated with the study of chromatic harmony.

▓ ▓ ▓ Skips larger than one octave are found in the next four melodies.

234. *Allegro*

235. *Allegro moderato*

236. *Andante con moto*

237. *Allegro deciso*

238. *Allegro con brio*

239. *Andante ed espressivo*

240. *Largo e mesto*

241. *Lively*

242. *Larghetto*

243. *Mit Kraft*

244. *Allegro gioviale*

245. *Valse* (in one)

246. *Allegro grazioso*

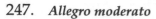 Skips to chromatic notes are introduced in the next five melodies.

247. *Allegro moderato*

248. *Andante mosso*

249. *Tempo di valse*

250. *Larghetto*

251. *Moderato*

252. *Gavotte*

253. *Pas trop lent*

254. *Largo e maestoso*

255. *Allegretto*

256. *Andante con moto*

257. *Fast*

258. *Sostenuto ed espressivo*

259. *Allegretto*

260. *Schnell und fröhlich*

261. *Largo*

262. *Vivace*

263. *Etwas langsam und zart*

264. *Allegro deciso*

265. *Briskly*

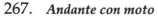 Secondary dominants are outlined in the next five melodies.

266. *Energetic*

267. *Andante con moto*

268. *Allegro*

269. *Sehr rasch*

270. *Allegretto*

271. *Innig*

272. *Valse*

273. *Ziemlich bewegt*

274. *Allegretto*

The meters $\frac{5}{8}$ and $\frac{5}{4}$ are introduced in the next five melodies.

275. *Allegro*

276. *Andantino*

277. *Allegro*

278. *Slowly and simply*

279. *Moderate*

280. *Lento*

281. *Presto*

282. *Lilting*

283. *Andantino amabile*

284. *Lebhaft*

285. *Allegretto*

286. *Animé et très expressif*

287. *Allegro assai*

288. *Presto alla Tarantella*

289. *Cheerful*

290. *Assez lent*

291. *Medium bounce*

292. *Andante espressivo*

293. *Rather slowly*

294. *Vif et léger*

295. *Modéré et doucement*

The next four melodies, in the major mode, include the flatted sixth scale degree.

296. *Andante*

297. *Andantino*

298. *Waltz*

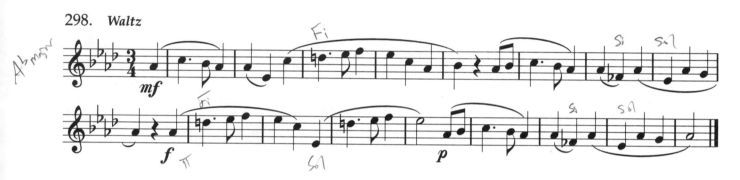

299. *Andante semplice*

300. *Quasi presto*

The dominant ninth chord, in both major and minor, is outlined in the next four melodies.

306. *Andante*

307. *Larghetto*

308. *Andantino*

309. *Adagio ed espressivo*

310. *Largo*

311. *Allegretto scherzoso*

315. **Ballando**

316. **Allegretto e leggiero**

317. **Galop**

318. **Lento assai**

319. *Fast*

320. *Allegretto*

321. *Il più presto possibile*

322. *Valse*

327. *Allegretto*

328. *Lively*

329. *Vif et gai*

330. **Etwas langsam und zart**

331. **In jig time**

332. **Allegro assai**

333. *Mässig und ausdrucksvoll*

334. *Allegro non troppo*

335. *Fast*

336. *Energetic*

337. *Largo con affetto*

338. *Presto*

FM

MELODIES ▦ SECTION IV

To be used with Section IV of all other chapters

The melodies in this section present challenging problems of intonation, rhythm, and phrase structure. The tenor clef is introduced at the beginning of the section. Modulation to remote keys, the use of augmented and diminished intervals, a more intensified chromaticism, modal idioms, and complex syncopation offer the advanced student both challenge and stimulus.

The concluding melodies of this section introduce twentieth-century idioms.

▦ ▦ ▦ The next nine melodies are written using the tenor clef.

339. *Allegro*

340. *Moderato*

341. *Largo*

342. *Andante*

343. *Allegro*

344. *Sostenuto*

345. *Presto*

346. *Allegro deciso*

347. *Allegretto*

348. *Lento*

349. *Minuet*

350. *Tempo di valzer*

351. *Avec mouvement*

352. *Con spirito*

353. *Lento*

354. *Con moto*

355. *Allegretto giocoso*

356. *Lento*

357. *Valse brillante* (in one)

358. *Molto adagio*

359. *Slow and expressive*

360. *Andante misterioso*

361. *Sostenuto ed espressivo*

362. *Andantino e leggiero*

363. *Moderato con moto*

364. *Langsam und ausdrucksvoll*

365. *Allegro energico*

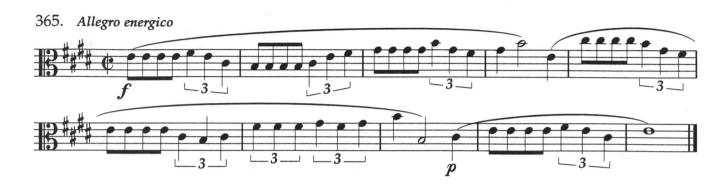

366. *Allegro assai*

367. *Bewegt*

  The flatted supertonic scale degree is introduced in the next five melodies.

368. *Andante*

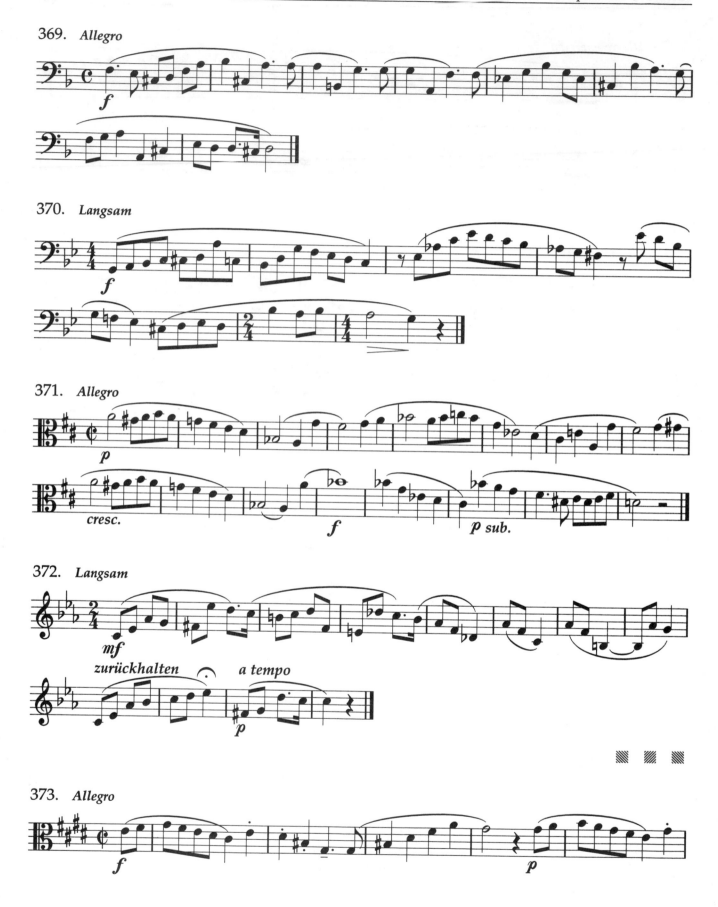

374. Moderato e pomposo

375. Larghetto

376. Allegretto

386. *Andante con moto*

387. *Free and easy*

388. *Ländler*

389. *Valse brillante*

390. **Etwas gedehnt**

391. **Allegro**

392. **Allegro deciso**

393. **Andantino**

394. *Arietta—Andante*

395. *With movement*

396. *Andante*

397. *With gusto*

398. *Grave*

399. *Lento ed espressivo*

400. *Allegro piacevole*

▨ ▨ ▨   The next four melodies include changing meters.

401. *Allegro*

402. **Langsam**

403. **Lebhaft**

404. **Piacevole**

405. **Allegro energico**

406. *Allegretto*

407. *Andantino espressivo*

408. *Allegro moderato*

409. *Très vif et détaché*

410. *Allegro*

411. *Maestoso*

412. *Larghetto*

413. *Allegro non troppo*

414. *Lebhaft und fröhlich*

415. *Allegro con brio*

416. *Allegretto*

417. *Presto leggiero*

418. *Allegro piacevole*

419. *Lento*

420. *Moderato e mesto*

421. *Largo espressivo*

422. *Slow Blues*

427. *Tempo di marcia*

Major and minor modes are combined in the next seven melodies.

428. *Allegro con spirito*

429. *Allegretto*

430. *With well-marked rhythm*

431. *Bewegt*

432. *Allegro*

433. *Allegro non tanto*

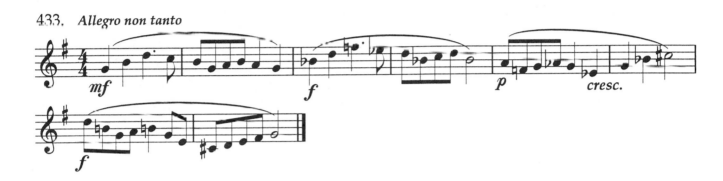

434. *Tempo di minuetto*

435. *Expressively*

440. *Con moto*

441. *With spirit*

442. *Lively*

443. *Spiritoso*

444. *Allegro gioviale*

445. *Lebhaft und stark*

446. *Andante espressivo*

447. *Allegro*

448. *Allegro giocoso*

449. *Vivo*

450. *Allegro marcato*

451. *Andante*

452. *Allegro moderato*

453. *Andante*

454. *Moderato*

Octatonic scales have eight notes arranged in a pattern of alternating whole steps and half steps. Two octatonic scales:

The next four melodies are based on octatonic scales.

455. *Andante con moto*

456. *Flowing*

457. *Andante espressivo*

458. *Allegretto gioviale*

459. *Allegretto*

460. *Vivo*

461. *Allegro con brio*

▨ CHAPTER TWO ▧

Duets

The experience of singing one part while listening to another develops that sense of independence so essential to a good ensemble performer. Hearing the harmonic and contrapuntal relation between your melodic line and another will help maintain correct intonation and rhythmic precision. For additional practice, it is useful to play one part at the piano while singing the other. These duets may also be used for dictation.

DUETS ▦ *SECTION I*

1. *Andante*

2. *Allegretto*

3. *Lento*

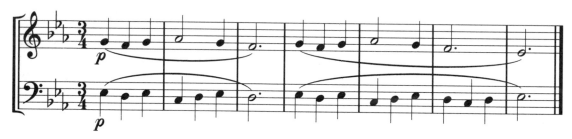

4. *Andantino*

5. *Larghetto*

106

6. *Andante*

7. *Larghetto*

8. *Allegretto*

9. *Andante*

10. *Allegro*

11. *Allegretto*

12. *Andante*

13. *Allegretto*

14. *Moderato con moto*

15. *Andante*

16. *Andante cantabile*

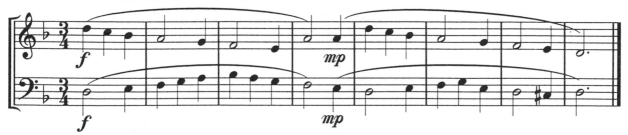

17. *Larghetto*

18. *Allegro moderato*

19. *Allegretto*

20. *Allegro*

21. *Allegro con spirito*

22. *Moderato con moto*

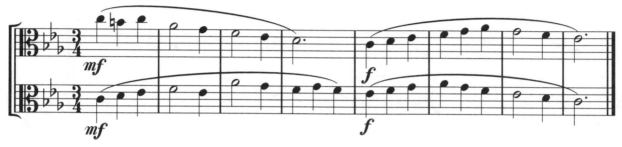

23. *Allegro giocoso*

24. *Allegro*

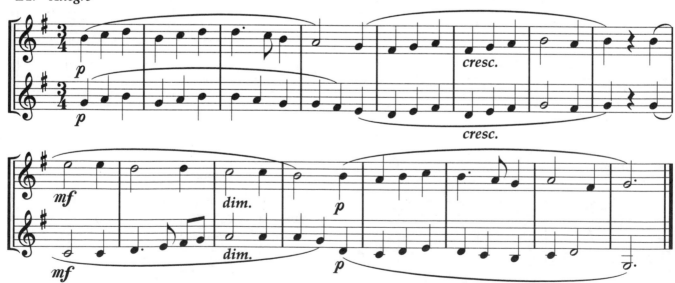

25. *Allegretto*

26. *Allegro moderato*

27. *Allegretto*

28. *Andante espressivo*

29. *Allegretto*

30. *Andante con moto*

DUETS ▨ *SECTION II*

31. *Andante con moto*

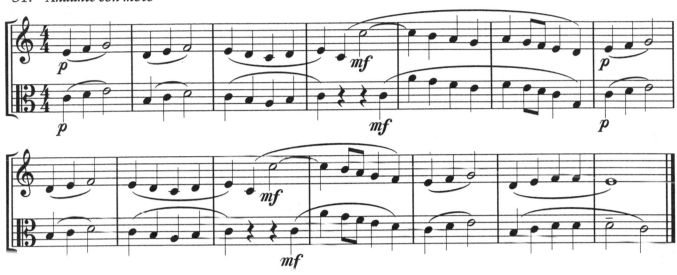

32. *Andantino*

113

33. *Andantino*

34. *Langsam*

35. *Largo espressivo*

36. *Lento*

37. *Andante espressivo*

38. *Giocoso*

39. *Mässig*

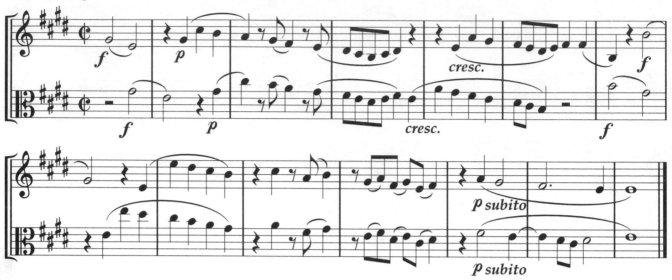

40. *Allegro con spirito*

41. *Andantino*

42. *En allant*

43. *Adagio espressivo*

44. *Andante cantabile*

45. *Allegretto giocoso*

46. *Moderato*

51. *Allegretto*

f (la seconda volta *p*)

52. *Flowing*

53. *Allegro*

54. *Andantino*

57. *Allegretto*

58. *Con brio*

59. *Andante con moto*

60. *Andantino* **(Dorian)**

61. *Ben ritmico* **(Phrygian)**

DUETS ▓ **SECTION III**

65. *Gedehnt*

66. *Vivo*

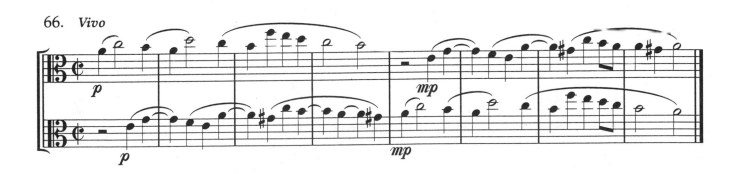

67. *Allegro*

68. *Langsam*

69. *Andante con moto*

70. *Vivo*

71. *Moderato con tenerezza*

72. *Molto allegro*

73. *Vif et gai*

74. *Lively*

75. *Lively, with humor*

76. *Allegro moderato*

77. *Spiritoso*

78. *Allegretto*

79. *Adagietto*

80. *Largo*

83. **Langsam und ausdrucksvoll**

84. **Allegro molto**

85. *Allegro deciso*

86. *Andante espressivo*

87. *Mässig*

88. *Etwas langsam*

89. *Affettuoso*

calando

calando

90. *Allegro deciso*

f sempre

f sempre

91. *Merrily*

92. *Adagietto*

93. *Andante*

94. *Ziemlich langsam*

95. *Andante con moto*

96. *Gedehnt*

97. *Andante*

98. *Andante espressivo*

99. *Molto lento*

100. *Deciso*

101. *Allegretto e marcato*

102. *March*

▨ CHAPTER THREE ▧

Sing and Play

These exercises provide an introductory experience in singing vocal music with piano accompaniment. This chapter deals with the same melodic issues as are found in Chapter One, now with accompaniment; each section ends with a series of themes and variations for voice and piano.

These short pieces should be sung and played by the same person. Therefore the piano parts have been kept at a minimal level of difficulty. The emphasis is on the melodic line and its relationship to the accompaniment. The piano is especially useful in overcoming potential difficulties with intonation. Students with little pianistic ability may use the duets of Chapter Two as additional easy sing and play exercises. We suggest that a number of these exercises be assigned each week prior to the class meeting.

The skill acquired through the study of this chapter will prepare the student to explore some of the richest treasures in the musical literature.

SING AND PLAY ▓ *SECTION I*

1. *Moderato*

2. *Andante*

3. *Moderato*

4. *Allegro*

5. *Andante*

142

6. *Allegro*

7. *Allegro*

8. *Andante sostenuto*

9. *Largo*

10. *Andante*

11. *Allegro*

12a. *Allegro* (**maggiore**)

12b. *Allegro* (**minore**)

13. *Allegretto*

14. *Andante*

15. *Allegretto*

16. *Andante*

17. *Allegro*

18. *Allegretto*

19. *Allegro*

20. *Moderato*

21. *Andante*

22a. *Andante* (maggiore)

22b. *Andante* (minore)

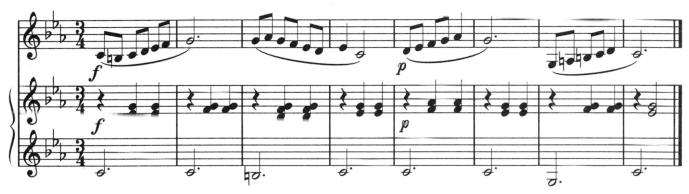

23a. *Andantino* (maggiore)

23b. *Andantino* (minore)

24. *Allegretto*

25. *Moderato*

26. *Allegro*

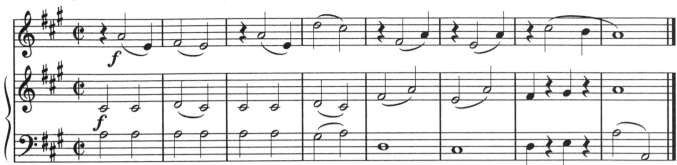

27a. *Moderato* (**maggiore**)

27b. *Moderato* (**minore**)

28. *Allegretto*

29a. *Allegro* **(maggiore)**

29b. *Allegro* **(minore)**

Themes and Variations for Voice and Piano

The following exercises provide further opportunity for combining voice and piano. Variation procedures illustrate a variety of piano textures, harmony, and rhythms in support of the vocal lines.

30. Theme: *Allegro*

Var. I: *Allegro*

Var. II: *Andante*

Var. III: *Andante*

Var. IV: *Allegro molto*

31.   **Theme:** *Allegro deciso*

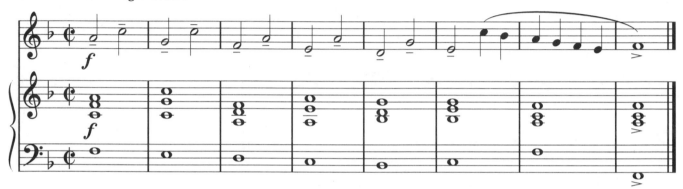

Var. I: *Allegretto*

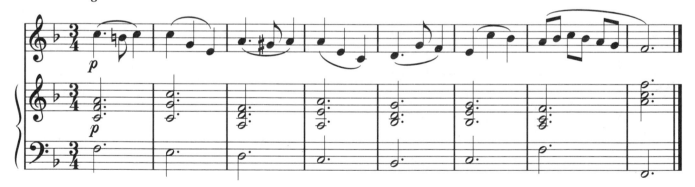

Var. II: *Moderato*

Var. III: *Presto*

Var. IV: *March*

32. Theme: *Andante sostenuto*

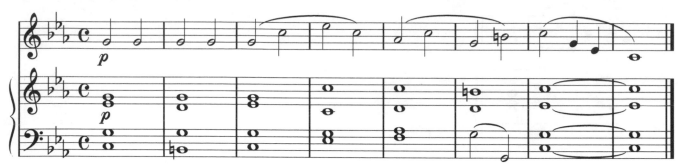

Var. I: *Moderato*

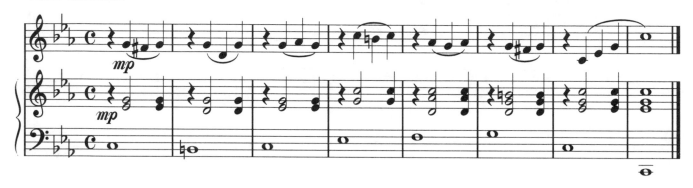

Var. II: *Adagio*

Var. III: *Allegro*

Var. IV: *Allegro*

Var. V: *Moderato*

33. *Moderato*

34. *Andantino*

35. *Allegro*

36. *Allegretto*

37. *Andantino*

38. *Lento*

39. *Moderato*

40. *Allegretto*

41. *Allegretto*

42. *Andantino*

43a. *Moderato* (**maggiore**)

43b. *Moderato* (**minore**)

44. *Andante*

45a. *Modéré* **(maggiore)**

45b. *Modéré* **(minore)**

46. *Allegro*

47a. *Moderato* (**maggiore**)

47b. *Moderato* (**minore**)

48. *Allegro*

49. *Lento*

50. *Lento*

51. *Allegro*

52a. *Andantino* (**maggiore**)

52b. *Andantino* (**minore**)

53. *Andante*

54. *Moderato*

55. *Allegretto*

59. *Adagio*

60. *Allegro*

61. *Langsam*

62. *Andante*

63. *Moderato*

64. *Adagio*

65. *Andante cantabile*

66. *Allegretto*

67. *Adagietto*

Themes and Variations for Voice and Piano

68.   **Theme:** *Moderato*

Var. I: *Moderato*

Var. II: *Allegro*

Var. III: *Allegro*

Var. IV: *Andante*

Var. V: *Allegro tranquillo*

69. **Theme:** *Mesto*

Var. I: *Andante*

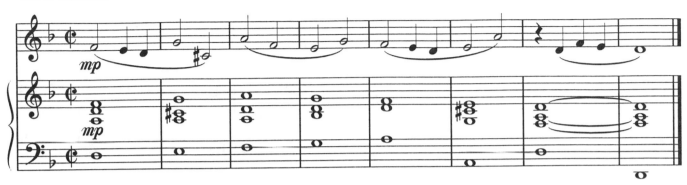

Var. II: *Moderato*

Var. III: *Andantino*

Var. IV: *Allegretto*

Var. V: *Lento*

70. Theme: *Allegro grazioso*

Var. I: *Allegro*

Var. II: *Adagio*

Var. III: *Allegro gioviale*

Var. IV: *Moderato*

Var. V: *Allegro*

71. **Theme:** *Allegro*

Var. I: *Allegro*

Var. II: *Moderato*

Var. III: *Andante espressivo*

Var. IV: *Allegro*

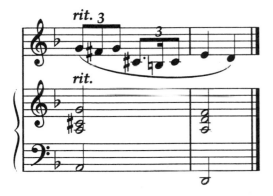

72a. *Allegro assai* (**maggiore**)

72b. *Allegro assai* (**minore**)

73. *Allegretto*

76. *Andante con moto*

77. *Allegretto grazioso*

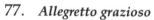

78. *Largo*

79. *Allegretto*

80a. *Moderato* (**maggiore**)

80b. *Moderato* **(minore)**

81. *Pastorale*

82. *Etwas bewegt*

83. *Mässig und zart*

84. *Andantino*

85. *Langsam*

*Appoggiatura: see *Glossary*.

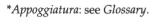

86. *Slowly*

87. *Larghetto*

88. **Berceuse**

89. **Mässig und ausdrucksvoll**

90. *Andante maestoso*

91. *Andantino*

92. *Andante cantabile*

93. *Recitativo*

Themes and Variations for Voice and Piano

94.   **Theme:** *Allegro grazioso*

Var. I: *Moderato*

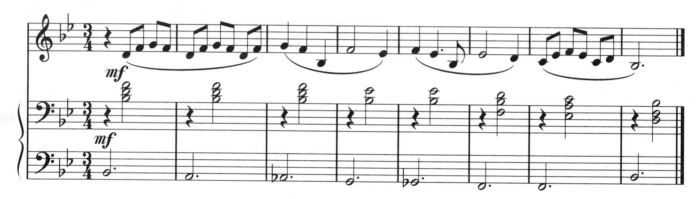

Var. II: *Gioviale*

Var. III: *Cantabile*

Var. IV: *Andante espressivo*

Var. V: *Brillante*

95. **Theme:** *Slow blues*

Var. I: *Moderato*

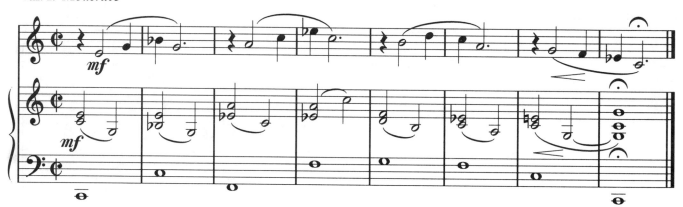

Var. II: *With energy*

Var. III: *Lazy*

Var. IV: *Moderately fast*

Var. V: *Jazz waltz*

96. **Theme:** *Ruhig*

Var. I: *Walzer*

Var. II: *Lebhaft*

Var. III: *Ziemlich langsam*

Var. IV: *Walzer*

Var. V: *Ruhig*

97.   **Theme:** *Slow and hymnlike*

Var. I: *Slow and solemn*

Var. II: *Lively*

Var. III: *Fast*

Var. IV: *Very slow*

Var. V: *Slow and solemn*

98. **Theme:** *Adagio e sostenuto*

Var. I: *Moderato*

Var. II: *Andante espressivo*

Var. III: *Gioviale*

Var. IV: *L'istesso tempo*

Var. V: *Innocente*

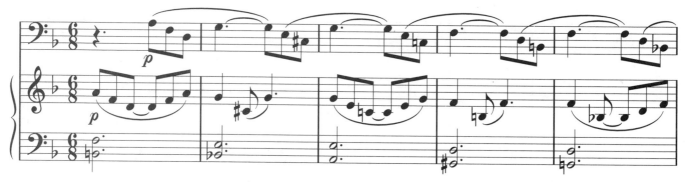

99. *Innig*

100. *Andante sostenuto*

101. *Mit Empfindung*

102. *Moderately fast*

*The rhythm ♫ in classical music is usually performed as ♪³♪ in jazz.

105. Vivo

106. *Andante con moto*

107. *Ziemlich langsam*

108. *Lento*

109. *Slowly* ♩ = 72

110. *Teneramente*

111. *Andantino con grazia*

112. *Allegro con brio*

113. *Pensive* ♩ = 66

114. *Moderate*

115. *Slow*

116. *Tenderly*

117. *Moderately slow*

118. *Andante con moto*

119. *Energetic, but not too fast*

120. *Slowly*

121. *Slow and expressive*

122. *Jazz waltz* **(in one)**

123. *Doux et expressif*

124. *Molto sostenuto*

125. *Modéré*

126. *Lentement*

127. *Ruhig* ♩ = 60

128. *Langsam* ♩ = 54

Themes and Variations for Voice and Piano

129. **Theme:** *Appassionato*

Var. IV: *Moderato*

Var. V: *Allegro grazioso*

130. **Theme:** *Slow blues*

Var. I: *Jazz waltz* **(in one)**

Var. II: *Flowing*

Var. III: *With energy*

Var. IV: *With excitement*

131. Theme: *Playfully*

Var. I: *Slow*

Var. II: *Agitated*

Var. III: *Slow and solemn*

Var. IV: *Slowly and expressively*

132.   **Theme:** *Adagio sostenuto*

Var. I: *Grave*

Var. II: *Piacevole*

Var. III: *Adagio*

Var. IV: *Funerale*

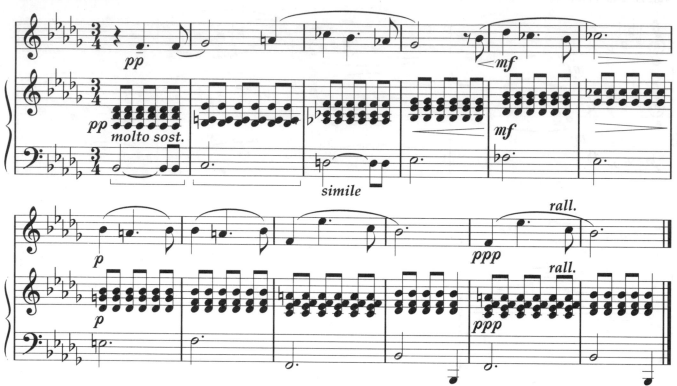

133.   **Theme:** *Andante*

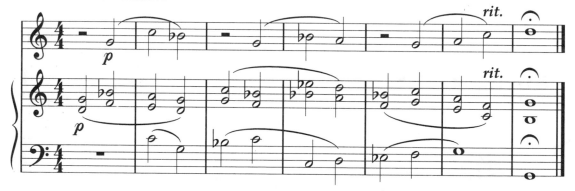

Var. I: *Moderato*

Var. II: *Allegretto*

Var. III: *Andante*

Var. IV: *Allegro* (**in one**)

Var. V: *Maestoso*

134.   **Theme:** *Lent*

Var. I: *Modéré*

Var. II: *Gracieux*

Var. III: *Léger*

Var. IV: *Lentement*

Var. V: *Gracieux*

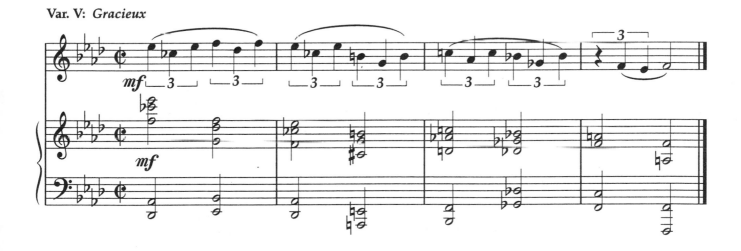

CHAPTER FOUR

Themes and Variations (Unaccompanied)

Themes and variations provide the opportunity of singing more extended musical compositions. The constantly changing character of the music as the variations unfold demands a larger range of interpretive skills than the shorter melodies of Chapter One.

The nature of the material and the levels of difficulty are comparable to those of the melodies in Chapter One.

THEMES AND VARIATIONS (UNACCOMPANIED)
SECTION I

1st Theme and Variations

2nd Theme and Variations

Theme: *Moderato*

Var. I: *Andante*

Var. II: *Allegro*

Var. III: *Presto*

Var. IV: *Lento*

Var. V: *Allegro con brio*

3rd Theme and Variations

Theme: *Andante*

Var. I: *Andante*

Var. II: *Andantino*

Var. III: *Lento*

Var. IV: *Andante* (**maggiore**)

Var. V: *Allegretto* (**minore**)

4th Theme and Variations

Theme: *Allegro moderato*

Var. I: *Allegro*

Var. II: *Andantino*

Var. III: *Allegro*

Var. IV: *Tempo I*

Var. V: *Allegro con spirito*

5th Theme and Variations

Theme: *Moderato*

Var. I: *Moderato*

Var. II: *Poco più mosso*

Var. III: *Largo* (minore)

Var. IV: *Allegretto* (maggiore)

Var. V: *Allegro*

THEMES AND VARIATIONS (UNACCOMPANIED)
SECTION II

6th Theme and Variations

Theme: *Allegro innocente*

Var. I: *Grazioso*

Var. II: *Andantino*

Var. III: *Andante*

Var. IV: *Adagietto (minore)*

Var. V: *Allegretto (maggiore)*

7th Theme and Variations

Theme: *Lento*

Var. I: *Un poco più mosso*

Var. II: *Andantino*

Var. III: *Allegretto*

Var. IV: *Adagio* **(maggiore)**

Var. VI *Allegro gioviale* **(minore)**

Var. VI: *Allegro*

8th Theme and Variations

Theme: *Moderato*

Var. I: *Moderato*

Var. II: *Allegretto*

Var. III: *Un poco sostenuto*

Var. IV: *Largo* (minore)

Var. V: *Allegro non troppo* (maggiore)

9th Theme and Variations

Theme: *Adagietto*

Var. I: *Alla marcia*

Var. II: *Allegretto*

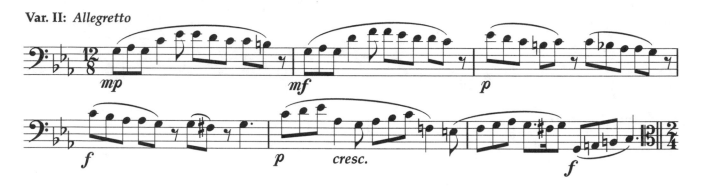

Var. III: *Allegro misterioso*

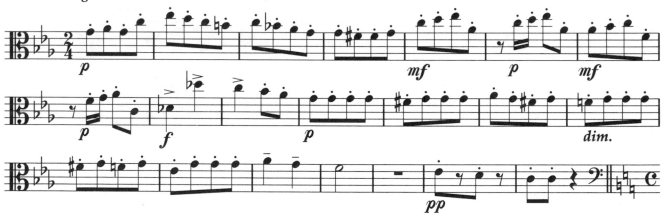

Var. IV: *Largo e cantabile* (**maggiore**)

Var. V: *Valse brillante* **(minore)**

THEMES AND VARIATIONS (UNACCOMPANIED)
▦ SECTION III

10th Theme and Variations

Theme: *Allegro grazioso*

Var. I: *Più allegro*

Var. II: *Un poco più mosso*

Var. III: *Allegro (minore)*

Var. IV: *Allegro con moto* (maggiore)

248

Var. V: *Tempo di valzer*

Var. VI: *Allegro*

11th Theme and Variations

Theme: *Allegretto grazioso*

Var. I: *Allegretto*

Var. II: *Larghetto* **(minore)**

Var. III: *Adagietto* **(maggiore)**

Var. IV: *Allegro molto*

Var. V: *Allegro scherzando*

12th Theme and Variations

Theme: *Andante*

Var. I: *Andantino*

Var. II: *Allegro appassionato*

Var. III: *Andante tranquillo* (maggiore)

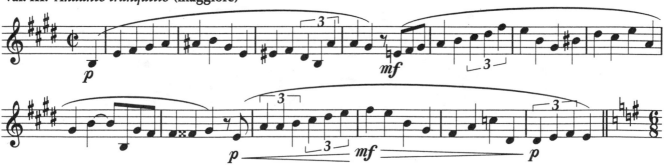

Var. IV: *Allegretto* (**minore**)

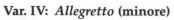

Var. V: *Vivace*

13th Theme and Variations

Theme: *Andante cantabile*

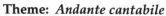

Var. I: *Un poco più sostenuto*

Var. II: *Allegro*

Var. III: *Allegro deciso*

Var. IV: *Poco adagio*

Var. V: *Allegro spiritoso*

THEMES AND VARIATIONS (UNACCOMPANIED)
SECTION IV

14th Theme and Variations

Theme: *Vivace*

Var. I: *Allegretto*

Var. II: *Andantino* (minore)

Var. III: *Allegretto*

Var. IV: *Allegro (maggiore)*

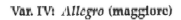

15th Theme and Variations

Theme: *Allegretto*

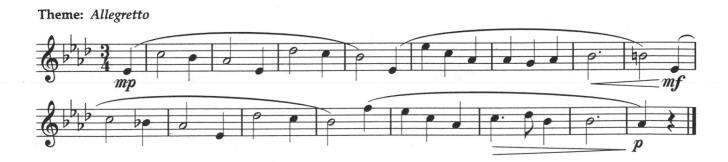

Var. I: *Andante*

Var. II: *Grazioso*

Var. III: *Allegro* **(minore)**

Var. IV: *Andantino cantabile* **(maggiore)**

Var. V: *Moderato*

Var. VI: *Allegro*

16th Theme and Variations

Theme: *Andante*

Var. I: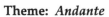

Var. II: *Un poco meno mosso* (maggiore)

Var. III: *Moderato* (minore)

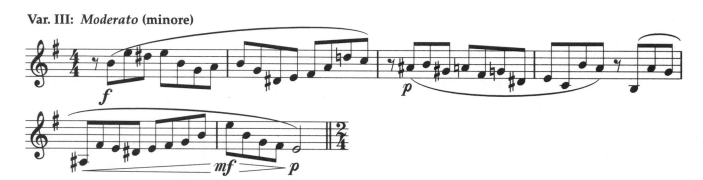

Var. IV: *Allegro*

17th Theme and Variations

Theme: *Allegro deciso*

Var. I: *Allegretto*

Var. II: *Allegro*

Var. III: *Moderato* **(minore)**

Var. IV: *Presto* **(maggiore)**

CHAPTER FIVE

Melodies from the Literature

The melodies of Chapter Five come from two sources: the concert repertory of the last two and a half centuries, and the literature of folk music from many lands. These melodies offer a wide diversity of styles, as well as many different approaches to matters of phrasing, dynamics, and interpretation.

Many of the melodies have been edited to conform with the phrasing and articulation of the melodies in previous chapters. Some have been adapted to make them more suitable for sight singing. The four sections of this chapter are coordinated with the sections of the previous chapters.

260

MELODIES FROM THE LITERATURE ▨ SECTION I

1. Moderato — Chorale: "Christus, der ist mein Leben"

2. Largo — Chorale: "Weg, mein Herz, mit den Gedenken"

3. Andante — Chorale: "Wie schön leuchtet der Morgenstern"

4. Langsam — Chorale: "Ach, wie nichtig, ach, wie flüchtig"

5. Larghetto — Chorale: "In allen meinen Taten"

6. *Andante con moto*   **Chorale: "Herzliebster Jesu, was hast du?"**

7. *Moderato*   **Chorale: "Straf' mich nicht in deinem Zorn"**

8. *Allegro*   **Beethoven: Violin Concerto, I**

9. *Marchlike*   **Germany**

10. *Allegretto*   **Germany**

11. *Slow*　　　　　　　　　　　　　　　　　　　　**Appalachia, USA**

12. **With Spirit**　　　　　　　　　　　　　　　　　**Appalachia, USA**

13. *Allegro*　　　　　　　　　　　　　　　　　　　　　　**Sweden**

14. *Vivace*　　　　　　　　　　　　　　　　　　　　　　**Sweden**

21. *Langsam*   Schubert: Wiegenlied

22. *Allegro assai*   Beethoven: Symphony No. 9 ("Choral"), IV

23. *Lustig*   Germany

24. *Fast*   Appalachia, USA

25. *Mässig*   Germany

26. *Fast and lively*   H. C. Work: "Kingdom Coming"

27. *Allegretto*   Mozart: *The Marriage of Figaro,* Act I

28. *Moderato*   Japan

29. *Very slowly*   Japan

30. *Langsam*   Chorale: "O Haupt voll Blut und Wunden"

31. *Slow* Spiritual

32. *Andante con moto* Mendelssohn: Symphony No. 4 ("Italian"), II

33. *Lively* Spiritual

34. *Moderato* J. Bland: "Oh, Dem Golden Slippers"

35. *Fast* Afrikaans

36. *Andante*   **Mozart:** *Don Giovanni*, **Act I**

37. *Moderato*   **J. Bland: "Carry Me Back to Old Virginny"**

38. *Moderato*   **Foster: "Maggie By My Side"**

39. *Slowly and expressively*   **Appalachia, USA**

40. *Slowly* Appalachia, USA

41. *Flowing* "Santa Lucia" (Italy)

42. *Allegretto* Denmark

43. *Adagio*

Verdi: **Prelude to** *La Traviata*

44. *Andante*

Japan

45. *Allegretto*

Russia

46. *Moderate*

Appalachia, USA

47. *Vivement*

France

48. *Allegro*

Handel: Concerto Grosso No. 12, II

49. *Moderate tempo, with sentiment*

Ireland

50. *Allegretto*

D. Scarlatti: Sonata in E♭ minor

51. *Very slowly*

Appalachia, USA

52. *Langsamer Ländler*

Germany

53. *Vif*

Rameau: *Le niais de Sologne*

54. *Allegretto*

Appalachia, USA

55. *Im Ländler-tempo* **Germany**

56. *March Tempo* **"Buffalo Gals" (USA)**

57. *Moderately fast* **"Captain Jinks" (USA)**

58. *Moderately fast* **Appalachia, USA**

59. *Sadly*   **Appalachia, USA**

60. *Plaintively*   **Spiritual**

61. *Frisch*   **Schumann: "Frühlings fahrt"**

62. *Andante*   **Bach: *Well-Tempered Clavier*, Book I, No. 1**

63. *Allegro*

Handel: *Judas Maccabeus*, Part III

64. *Leise*

Schumann: "Ich will meine Seele tauchen"

65. *Zart*

Germany

66. *Allegretto*

Beethoven: Symphony No. 6 ("Pastoral"), V

67. *Allegro*   **Vivaldi: Concerto Grosso, Op. 3, No. 11, II**

68. *Allegro ma non troppo*   **Dvořák: String Quartet, Op. 96, I**

69. *Allegro non troppo*   **Brahms: Symphony No. 1, IV**

70. *Andante*   **Mendelssohn: Symphony No. 3 ("Scottish"), I**

71. *Andantino quasi allegretto*   **Rimsky-Korsakov: *Scheherazade*, III**

72. *Tempo marziale*

Gounod: *Faust*, Act IV

73. ♩ = 100

Stravinsky: *Petrushka*, First Tableau

74. *Langsam*

Weber: *Der Freischütz*, Act II

75. *Allegro*

Haydn: Symphony No. 104 ("London"), I

76. *Allegro vivace*

Mozart: Symphony No. 41 ("Jupiter"), I

77. *Allegro vivace e con brio*   **Beethoven: Symphony No. 8, I**

78. *Andante con moto*   **Schubert: Symphony No. 5, II**

79. *Con grazia*   **Brahms: "Der Gang zum Liebchen"**

80. *Andante*   **Gluck:** *Orphée,* **Act III**

81. *Allegro moderato*   **Bach: "Little" Fugue**

82. *Largo*   Dvořák: Symphony No. 9 ("From The New World"), II

83. *Andantino*   Borodin: Polovetsian Dances from *Prince Igor*, Act II

84. *Andante tranquillo*   Mendelssohn: *Midsummer Night's Dream*, Nocturne

85. *Largo. Cantabile e mesto*   Haydn: String Quartet, Op. 76, No. 5, II

86. *Andante*   **Prokofiev:** *Lieutenant Kije Suite*

87. *Allegro*   **Mozart:** *The Marriage of Figaro,* **Act I**

88. *Andante con moto*   Beethoven: Symphony No. 5, II

89. *Con moto*   Hungary

90. *Allegro molto con brio*   R. Strauss: *Don Juan*

91. *Moderato cantabile*   Chopin: Fantasie-Impromptu

92. *Andantino* — Tchaikovsky: Symphony No. 4, II

93. *Moderato* — Prokofiev: *Peter and the Wolf*

94. *Allegro molto* — Beethoven: Symphony No. 3 ("Eroica"), IV

95. *Adagio un poco mosso* — Beethoven: Piano Concerto No. 5 ("Emperor"), II

96. *Allegretto*   Fauré: "Dans les ruines d'une abbaye"

97. *Moderato*   Foster: "Beautiful Dreamer"

98. *Très calme et doucement expressif*   Debussy: "The Girl with the Flaxen Hair"

99. *Andante moderato*   Beethoven: Symphony No. 9 ("Choral"), III

100. *Allegro cantabile*   **Liszt:** *Il Lamento*, I

101. *Allegro*   **Bach: Organ Fugue, BWV 542**

102. *Largo*   **Handel:** *Rinaldo*, **Act II**

103. *Nicht schnell*   **Schumann: "Marienwürmchen"**

104. *Allegro* **Berlioz:** *Roman Carnival Overture*

105. *Presto* **Haydn: Symphony No. 80, IV**

106. *Allegro* **Stravinsky:** *Petrushka,* **Third Tableau**

107. *Allegro giusto* **Stravinsky:** *Petrushka,* **First Tableau**

108. *Allegro ma non tanto*   **Beethoven: String Quartet, Op. 18, No. 4**

109. *Allegretto*   **Mozart: Clarinet Quintet, IV**

110. *Allegretto*   **Prokofiev: *Lieutenant Kije Suite***

111. *Moderato*   **Wagner: *Tannhäuser*, Act III**

112. *Allegro*

D. Scarlatti: Sonata in F minor

113. *Allegro agitato e presto*

Verdi: *Aida*, Act I

114. *Largo*

Verdi: *Il Trovatore*, Act II

115. *Andante con moto ♩ = 60*

Stravinsky: *The Rite of Spring*, Part II

116. *Andante con moto*

Mendelssohn: *Elijah*, Part I

117. *Largo*

Haydn: Symphony No. 88, II

118. *Andantino*

Saint-Saëns: *Samson and Delilah*, Act II

119. *Allegro*

Weber: Overture to *Oberon*

120. *Allegro fastoso*   **Prokofiev:** *Lieutenant Kije Suite*

121. *Sehr langsam und ausdrucksvoll*   **Brahms: "Die Mainacht"**

122. *Lebhaft*   **Schumann: "Und wüssten's die Blumen"**

123. *Langsam*   **Schumann: "Hör' ich das Liedchen klingen"**

124. *Allegro moderato*   **Bizet:** *Carmen,* **Act II**

125. *Allegretto maestoso*   **Rossini:** *Stabat Mater*

126. *Allegro vivace*   **Liszt:** *Mephisto Waltz*

127. *Poco allegretto*   **Brahms: Symphony No. 3, III**

128. *Ziemlich geschwind, doch kräftig*   Schubert: "Der stürmschen Morgen"

129. *Adagio*   Beethoven: Symphony No. 4, II

130. *Larghetto*   Bach: Mass in B Minor, Kyrie

131. *Andantino*   Tchaikovsky: *The Maid of Orleans*, Act I

132. M.M. ♩ = 112   Stravinsky: *L'Histoire du Soldat*

133. *Andantino*   **Fauré: "Après un rêve"**

134. *Allegretto dolcissimo*   **Grieg: "With a Violet"**

135. *Andante*   **Grieg: "Autumn Song"**

136. *Poco Allegro* Franck: Fugue

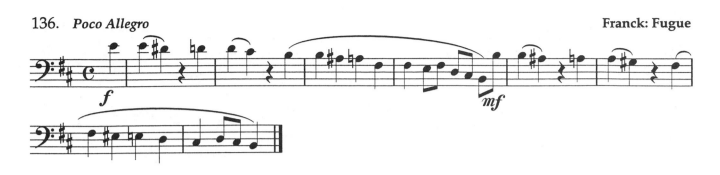

137. *Allegretto* Beethoven: Thirty-two Variations in C minor

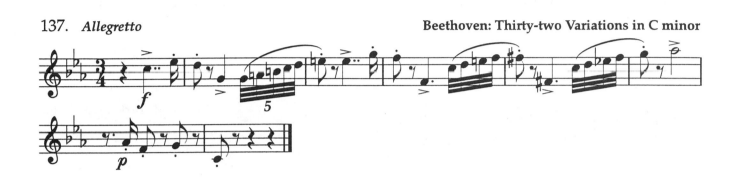

138. *Allegro* Mozart: Piano Concerto, K. 491, I

139. *Andantino* Prokofiev: *Peter and the Wolf*

140. *Allegro guisto e con forza*   **Musorgsky:** *Boris Godunov*, **Act I**

141. *Vivo ma non troppo*   **Chopin: Mazurka, Op. 7, No. 2**

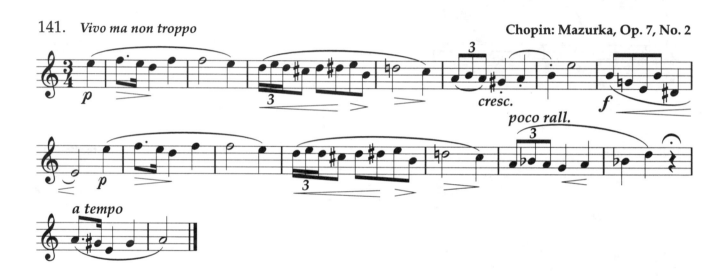

142. *Allegro energico*   **Liszt: Sonata**

143. *Andantino*

Rimsky-Korsakov: *Scheherazade*, II

144. M.M. ♩ = 168

Stravinsky: *The Firebird*

145. *Allegro*

Bach: Keyboard Concerto in D minor, I

146. *Lento*

Wagner: *Lohengrin*, Act I

147. *Andante sentimentale*

Tchaikovsky: Nocturne

148. *Larghetto, quasi largo*

Musorgsky: "Reverie"

149. *Mässig langsam*

Wagner: *Tristan und Isolde*, Act I

150. *Allegro molto*   **Wagner:** **Tannhäuser**

151. *Ruhig*   **Schoenberg:** *Transfigured Night*

152. *Allegro non troppo**   **Shostakovich: Symphony No. 1, I**

*Transposed up one tone for ease of singing.

153. *Lento*   **Bartók: Bagatelle, Op. 6, No. 6**

154. *Lento* ♩ = 50   **Stravinsky: *The Rite of Spring*, Part I**

Supplementary Exercises

These drills are designed to focus upon various technical problems. Part I is concerned principally with the development of the sense of key. Part II concentrates upon problems involving chromaticism. Both parts also contain rhythmic patterns arranged in order of increasing complexity. We suggest that the student first learn an exercise slowly and accurately, then increase the speed as much as possible.

SUPPLEMENTARY EXERCISES ▧ *PART I*

Exercises for Use with Sections I and II

▨ ▨ ▨ The first nine exercises focus on major scales and triads.

1.

2.

3.

4.

5.

6.

7.

8.

9.

▨ ▨ ▨ Exercises 10–13 are designed to show similarities and differences between the major and minor modes.

10a. Major

10b. Melodic minor

10c. Natural minor

10d. Harmonic minor

11a.   Major

11b.   Melodic minor

11c.   Natural minor

11d.   Harmonic minor

12a.

12b.

13a.

13b.

The next seven melodies focus on scales and triads in the minor mode.

14.

15.

16.

17.

18.

19.

31.

32.

33.

34.

35.

36.

37.

38.

39.

The next seven exercises stress specific intervals.

40.

41.

42.

43.

44.

45.

46.

47.

48.

49.

50.

51.

52.

53.

54.

The next eleven exercises start on a note other than the tonic.

68.

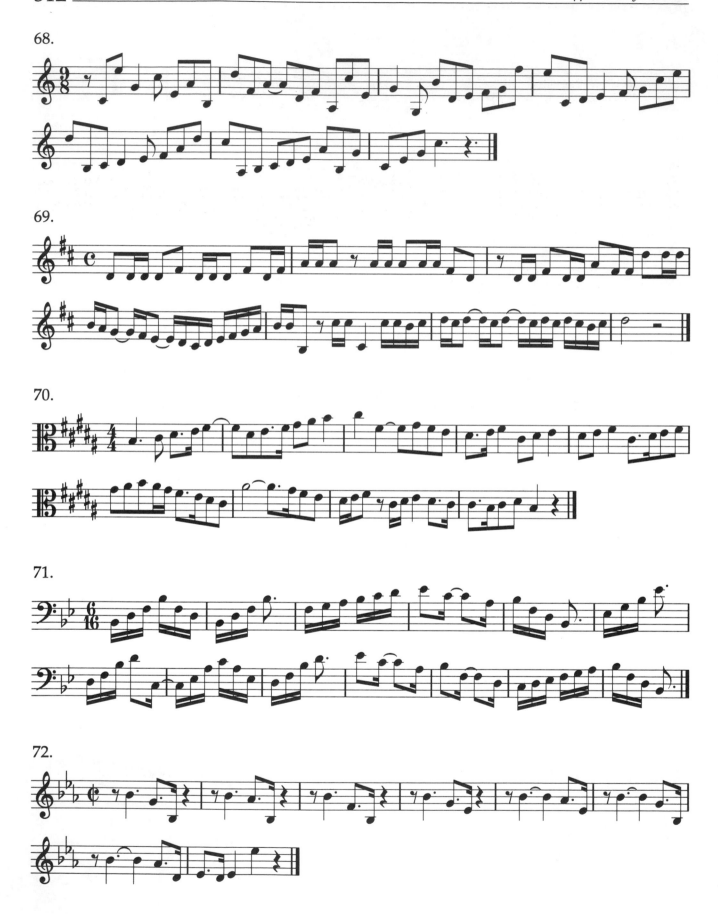

69.

70.

71.

72.

73.

74.

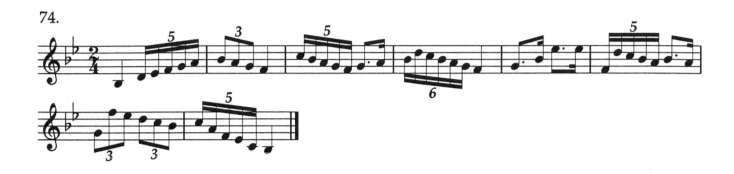

SUPPLEMENTARY EXERCISES ▨ *PART II*

Exercises for Use with Sections III and IV

▨ ▨ ▨ The next six exercises offer practice in enharmonic equivalents.

75.

76.

77.

78.

79.

80.

▨ ▨ ▨

Various scales and modes for practice.

81. Ionian mode (major scale)

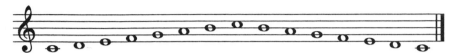

82. Aeolian mode (natural minor scale)

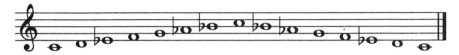

83. Harmonic minor scale

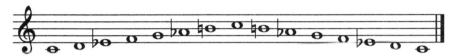

84. Melodic minor scale

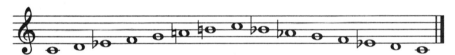

85. Dorian mode

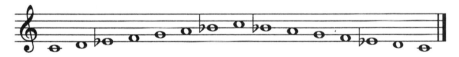

86. Mixolydian mode

87. Phrygian mode

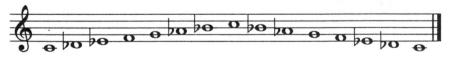

88. Locrian mode

89. Lydian mode

90. Whole-tone scale

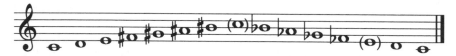

91. Chromatic scale

92a. Whole-tone and Chromatic scale

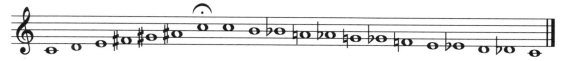

92b. Chromatic and Whole-tone scale

93.

94.

95.

96.

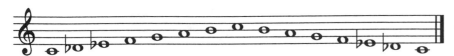

Octatonic scales have eight notes arranged in a pattern of alternating whole steps and half steps. Two octatonic scales:

97.

98.

The remaining exercises are studies in chromaticism.

99.

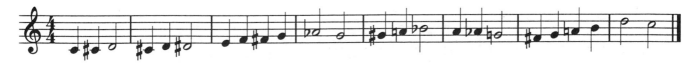

100.

101.

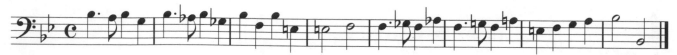

102.

103.

104.

105.

106.

107.

108.

109.

110.

111.

112.

113.

114.

115.

116.

117.

118.

119.

120.

121.

122.

123.

124.

125.

126.

127.

128.

129.

130.

131.

Glossary of Musical Terms

All terms are Italian unless otherwise noted. Abbreviations are given in parentheses.

Accelerando (accel.), gradually getting faster

Acciaccatura, a short appoggiatura

Adagietto, somewhat faster than adagio

Adagio, slow (slower than andante, faster than largo)

Affetto, tenderness

Affettuoso, tender

Agitato, agitated

Al fine, to the end

Alla, to the, at the, in the style of

Allargando, getting slower (crescendo often implied)

Allegretto, moderately fast (slower than allegro, faster than andante)

Allegro, fast, cheerful

All'ottava (8va), at the octave

Amabile, with love

Andante, moderately slow (slower than allegretto, faster than adagio)

Andantino, in modern usage, somewhat faster than andante; in older usage, somewhat slower than andante

Anima, spirit

Animato, animated, spirited

Animé, Fr., animated, spirited

A piacere, rhythm and tempo played at performer's discretion; freely

Appassionato, impassioned, intense

Appoggiatura, a melodic ornament; of the many types there are two main classifications: the *accented (long) appoggiatura* and the *short appoggiatura* (grace note). The first, written as a small note, is accented and borrows time value from the note it precedes. See note on page 186. The second is usually written as a small eighth or sixteenth note with a slanting stroke through the flag and stem. It is executed quickly, so that the accent falls on the melody note it precedes.

Arietta, a small aria

Assai, very

Assez, Fr., fairly, enough

A tempo, in the original speed

Attacca, attack or begin what follows without pause

Ausdrucksvoll, Ger., expressive

Avec, Fr., with

Ballando, dancing

Ben, well, very

Berceuse, Fr., lullaby

Bewegt, Ger., rather fast, agitated

Breit, Ger., broad, stately

Brillante, brilliant, sparkling

Brio, sprightliness, spirit

Calando, decreasing in both dynamics and tempo

Calma, Calmo, calm, tranquil

Calme, Fr., calm

Calore, warmth, passion

Cantabile, in a singing or vocal style

Cedez, Fr., slow down

Colla voce, literally "with the voice," meaning that the accompanist should follow the free rhythm used by the singer

Comodo, at a leisurely, convenient pace

Con, with

Corta, short

Crescendo (cresc.), increasing in volume of sound

Da capo (D. C.), from the beginning

Da capo al fine, repeat from the beginning to the end; that is, to the place where *fine* is written

Dal segno al fine, repeat from the sign to the end; that is, to the place where *fine* is written

Deciso, decisive, bold

Decrescendo (decresc.), decreasing in volume of sound
Del, of the
Détaché, Fr., detached
Di, of
Diminuendo (dim.), decreasing in volume of sound
Doch, Ger., yet
Dolce, sweet (*soft* is also implied)
Dolcissimo, very sweet
Doux, Fr., sweet (*soft* is also implied)
Doucement, Fr., sweet (*soft* is also implied)

E, ed, and
Eco, echo
Einfach, Ger., simple
Empfindung, Ger., expression
En allant, Fr., moving, flowing
Energico, energetic
Espressione, expression
Espressivo (espr.), expressive
Et, Fr., and
Etwas, Ger., somewhat
Expressif, Fr., expressive

Fastoso, stately, pompous
Feierlich, Ger., solemn
Feurig, Ger., fiery, impetuous
Fine, end
Fliessend, Ger., flowing
Force, Fr., strength, force
Forte (f), loud
Fortissimo (ff), very loud
Forza, force
Frisch, Ger., brisk, lively
Fröhlich, Ger., joyous, gay
Funèbre, funereal
Fuoco, fire, fiery

Gai, Fr., gay
Gaio, gay
Galop, Fr., a lively round-dance in duple meter
Gavotte, Fr., a French dance generally in common time, strongly accented, beginning on the third beat
Gedehnt, Ger., extended, sustained
Geschwind, Ger., quick
Gigue, Fr., a very fast dance of English origin in triple or sextuple meter
Giocoso, playful
Gioviale, jovial

Giusto, exact
Gracieux, Fr., graceful
Grave, very slow, solemn (generally indicates the slowest tempo)
Grazia, grace
Grazioso, graceful

Il più, the most
Im Zeitmass, Ger., in the original speed
Innig, Ger., heartfelt, ardent
Innocente, unaffected, artless

Kraft, Ger., strength
Kräftig, Ger., strong, robust

La, It. and Fr., the
Ländler, Ger., a country dance in triple meter
Langsam, Ger., slow
Larghetto, not as slow as largo
Largo, slow, broad
Lebhaft, Ger., lively, animated
Legato, to be performed with no interruption between tones; in a smooth and connected manner
Léger, Fr., light
Leggiero (also Leggero), light, delicate
Leise, Ger., soft
Lent, Fr., slow
Lentement, Fr., slowly
Lento, slow; not as slow as adagio
L'istesso tempo, in the same tempo as the previous section
Lunatico, performed in the spirit of lunacy
Lustig, Ger., cheerful

Ma, but
Maestoso, majestic, dignified
Maggiore, major (referring to mode)
Mais, Fr., but
Marcato, marked, with emphasis
Marcia, march
Marziale, martial
Mässig, Ger., moderate
Mazurka, Polish national dance in triple meter
Meno, less
Menuetto, minuet (moderately slow dance in triple meter)
Mesto, sad, mournful
Mezza voce, with half voice, restrained

Mezzo forte (**mf**), moderately loud

Mezzo piano (**mp**), moderately soft

Minore, minor (referring to mode)

Minuetto, minuet (moderately slow dance in triple meter)

Misterioso, mysterious

Mit, Ger., with

Moderato, moderate (slower than allegro, faster than andante)

Modéré, Fr., moderate (slower than allegro, faster than andante)

Möglich, Ger., possible

Molto, much, very

Morendo, dying away

Mosso, in motion (*più mosso*, faster; *meno mosso*, slower)

Moto, motion

Mouvement, Fr., motion, tempo, movement

Munter, Ger., lively

Nicht, Ger., not

Niente, nothing

Non, not

Ongarese, Hungarian

Pas, Fr., not

Pastorale, pastoral

Pedale, sustaining pedal on a piano

Perdendosi, gradually fading away

Pesante, heavy, ponderous

Peu, Fr., little

Piacere, at pleasure; expression is left to the performer's discretion

Piacevole, pleasant, graceful

Piano (**p**), soft

Pianissimo (**pp**), very soft

Più, more

Plus, Fr., more

Poco, little

Poco a poco, little by little, gradually

Pomposo, pompous

Portamento, a smooth gliding from one not to another

Possibile, possible

Pressez, Fr., press forward

Presto, very fast (faster than allegro)

Quasi, almost, nearly

Rallentando (*rall.*), gradually growing slower

Rasch, Ger., fast

Recitativo, sung in a declamatory manner

Retenu, Fr., held back

Rigore, strictness

Rigueur, Fr., strictness

Risoluto, firm, resolute

Ritardando (*rit.*), gradually growing slower

Ritenuto (*riten.*), held back

Ritmico, rhythmically

Rubato, literally, stolen; the term indicates freedom and flexibility of tempo so that the requirements of musical expression can be met

Ruhig, Ger., calm, tranquil

Saltarello, a lively dance of Italian origin, often in $\frac{9}{8}$

Sans, Fr., without

Scherzando, light, playful

Scherzo, a fast piece in triple meter

Scherzoso, jesting, playful

Schnell, Ger., fast

Seconda, second

Sehr, Ger., very

Semplice, simple, unaffected

Sempre, always

Sentimentale, It. and Fr., with sentiment

Senza fretta, without haste

Sforzando (**sf**, **sfz**), with force, accented

Siciliano, a moderately slow dance of pastoral character in $\frac{12}{8}$ or $\frac{6}{8}$ time

Simile, alike, in like manner

Smorzando, dying away

So, Ger., as

Sostenuto, sustained

Sotto voce, softly, with subdued voice

Spirito, spirit

Spiritoso, with spirit, animated

Staccato, detached

Stark, Ger., strong, vigorous

Stringendo, pressing forward

Subito (*sub.*), suddenly

Tanto, as much

Tarantella, a lively dance of Italian origin, usually in $\frac{6}{8}$

Tempo, time; refers to rate of motion

Tempo primo (*Tempo I*), in the original speed

Teneramente, tenderly, delicately

Tenerezza, tenderness

Tranquillo, tranquil

Très, Fr., very

Triste, It. and Fr., sad

Trop, Fr., too much, too
Troppo, too much, too

Un, It. and Fr., a
Und, Ger., and

Valse, Fr., waltz
Valzer, Ger., waltz
Vif, Fr., lively
Vite, Fr., quickly
Vivace, lively, quick
Vivement, Fr., lively
Vivo, lively, animated

Volta, turn or time

Walzer, Ger., waltz
Wie, Ger., as

Zart, Ger., tender, soft
Zeitmass, Ger., tempo
Ziemlich, Ger., somewhat, rather
Zu, Ger., too, to, by
Zuvor, Ger., previously
Zurückhalten, Ger., to hold back, to retard

Some Frequently Used Musical Signs

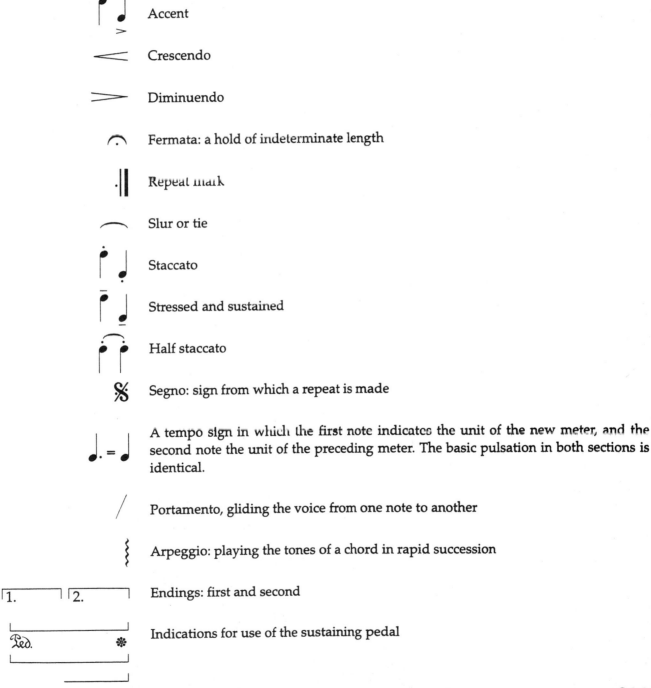

Accent

Crescendo

Diminuendo

Fermata: a hold of indeterminate length

Repeat mark

Slur or tie

Staccato

Stressed and sustained

Half staccato

Segno: sign from which a repeat is made

A tempo sign in which the first note indicates the unit of the new meter, and the second note the unit of the preceding meter. The basic pulsation in both sections is identical.

Portamento, gliding the voice from one note to another

Arpeggio: playing the tones of a chord in rapid succession

Endings: first and second

Indications for use of the sustaining pedal

329

Notes

Notes

Notes

Notes

Notes

Notes

Notes